# The Zetland Tunebook
## Volume One

Original Compositions and Arrangements
by
PM RW Lerwick

For the Great Highland Bagpipe
the
Lerwick Zetland Smallpipes
and
Other Scottish-System Smallpipes'

Published By The Shetland Piper
P.O. Box 22663, Robbinsdale, MN 55422-0663

Printed in Canada

ISBN O-9663321-1-3

# Table of Contents

## Original Compositions

Call to War ................................... page 9
Canadian Cool Front ..................... page 10
Cinders ........................................ page 11
The Clay Fish ............................... page 13
The Custudian .............................. page 14
Da BOMSKWAD ........................... page 15
Death Eats a Cracker .................... page 16
Depression ................................... page 18
Driving Home ............................... page 19
Farewell the Long Chanter ............ page 20
Going Out to Sea .......................... page 21
Hampster Slayer ........................... page 23
The Hand That Rocks the Cradle .... page 24
Hands Across the Water ................ page 25
Invercargill's Long Life .................. page 26
Invercargill's Long Life Seconds ...... page 27
Jimmy "Sticks" Moore .................... page 28
Johnny B Drone ............................ page 29
Kill the Whistler ............................ page 30
Little Blue Bike ............................. page 31
The Locker Room .......................... page 32
Master's Last ................................ page 33
The Mercury Slide ......................... page 34
Mike, It's Over .............................. page 35
Offhand Reel ................................ page 36
Old Runners ................................. page 37
The Pipe Major's Complaint ........... page 38
The Precipice ................................ page 40
The Precipice Seconds ................... page 41
Pudgy Mary .................................. page 42
Rain on the Roof ........................... page 43

Remote Control ............................. page 44
The Resignation ............................ page 45
The Resignation Seconds ............... page 46
Royal Red .................................... page 47
Season's End ................................ page 48
Season's End Seconds ................... page 49
Shetland Foxhunt .......................... page 50
Sodbusters ................................... page 51
The Tailor's Needle ....................... page 52
30+ ............................................. page 53
Tonka Bay .................................... page 54
The Top and Bottom Hand ............ page 55
Twisted Finger .............................. page 56
Wilting in the Sun ......................... page 57
Wring My Mop .............................. page 58

## Original Arrangements

Cork Hill ...................................... page 63
The Foxhunter ............................... page 64
The Foxhunter Seconds .................. page 65
Gilbert Clancy's Jig ....................... page 66
The Hairy Marriers ........................ page 67
The Hairy Marriers 1st Harmony .... page 68
The Hairy Marriers 2nd Harmony . page 69
High Level .................................... page 70
Highland Laddie ............................ page 71
Highland Laddie Seconds ............... page 72
Jock MacNichol's Fancy ................. page 73
Scotland the Brave ........................ page 74
Scotland the Brave Seconds ........... page 75

# Introduction

These tunes were scrawled sloppily on stray remnants of staff paper over the course of a few decades, starting soon after I first started piping. I was tempted to include cute anecdotes explaining their names and compositional history, but slapped myself brutally about the head and face with a half-frozen Alaskan king salmon until the idea left me.

Then I put the salmon on the barbecue.

Some of these tunes may look a bit thin in the "gracenote" department, but this isn't 1969, and the sole goal in modern piping isn't to prove you can cram more embellishments into the melody than the other guy. Many of these apparently "lobotomized" tunes are in fact meant to be cranked out on Lerwick Zetlands or other smallpipes at light-speed, and when played properly are in their own style harder than the embellishmentally overburdened, Victorian, executional gibberish you'll find in your favorite competition MSR or 6/8 march pulled out of the old regimental settings.

Another factor to note is that the various smallpipes favor the upperhand and generally have weaker lowerhand volume and tonal presentation, so when played on those instruments, many of these tunes and arrangements will suddenly display a "phantom" melody popping out of nowhere, which is not very present on the Highland pipe chanter because it does not favor the proper notes for the arrangement. "High Level" is the most obvious tune of this style in the collection. When played brightly as a straight-ahead Shetland-style reel, or in the Northumberland manic mode, the third part in particular does some amazingly cool rhythmic things you'll only hear in their fullness on the Zetlands.

These tunes are arranged in alphabetical order. This volume does not comprise necessarily my favorite or first tunes, nor is it indicative of any system of presentational priority at all concerning the relative worth of the tunes included. I simply started at the top of my aging pile of scribblings and went to work setting them up on computer until I had enough ready to make it worth publishing.

These tunes were laid out with EZ-SCORE+ on an Atari ST, and if you think the gracenotes should have been smaller, and you don't like the key signatures, hey, adjust. That's as small as the gracenotes get in the program, and I put the key signatures there on purpose so real musicians can also make sense of it if necessary. Sorry to confuse the pipers.

I've elected to notate the tunes in conventional Great Highland Bagpipe form in the key of A mixolydian, which is actually D major. The Zetlands play in D mixolydian. Scottish Smallpipes play in either A or D, but usually read and notate in A mixolydian. In any case, I've used the most universally understood Highland piper-based means of notational exchange, because again, most Highland pipers out there won't know what this paragraph means anyway, and this way at least they'll be able to read my music....

These tunes are printed one tune to a page, unless they exceed the length of a single page. This wastes some space, but conforms to the most useful format for the purposes of running through the photocopier and pirating off to the band and all your friends, which, if I've done my job, will be the ultimate destiny of this collection anyway.

R. W. Lerwick

My thanks to all the little people who made me what I am today.  (Whatever that may be.)

# Compositions

# Call to War

# Canadian Cool Front

10

# Cinders

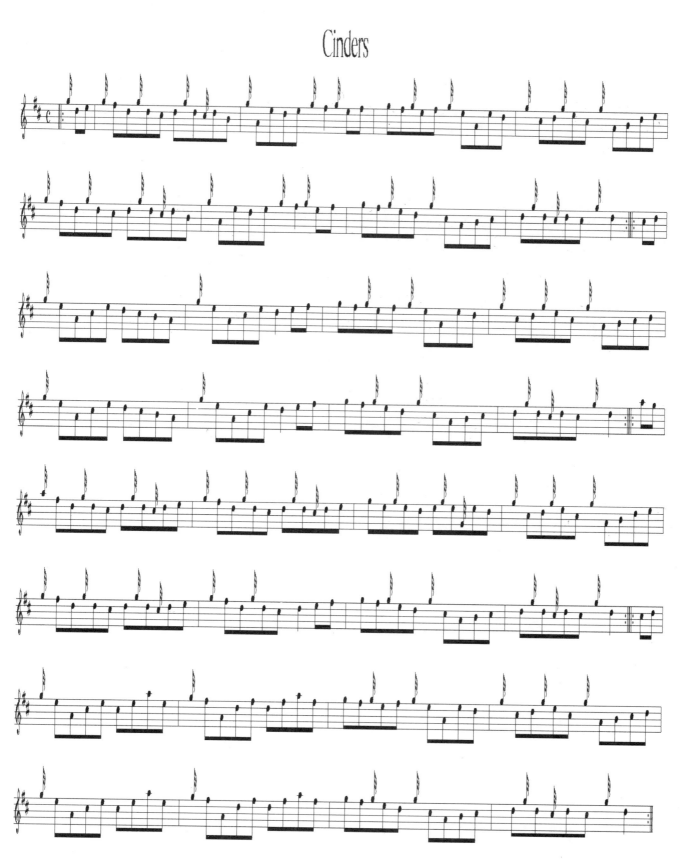

Cinders 5th/6th Parts

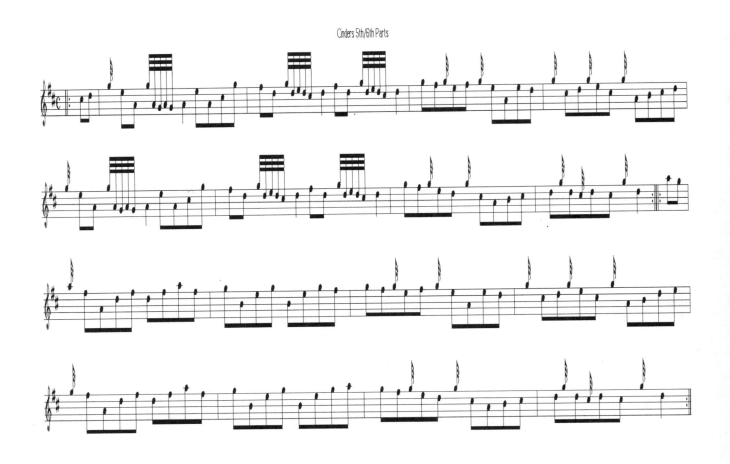

12

# The Clay Fish

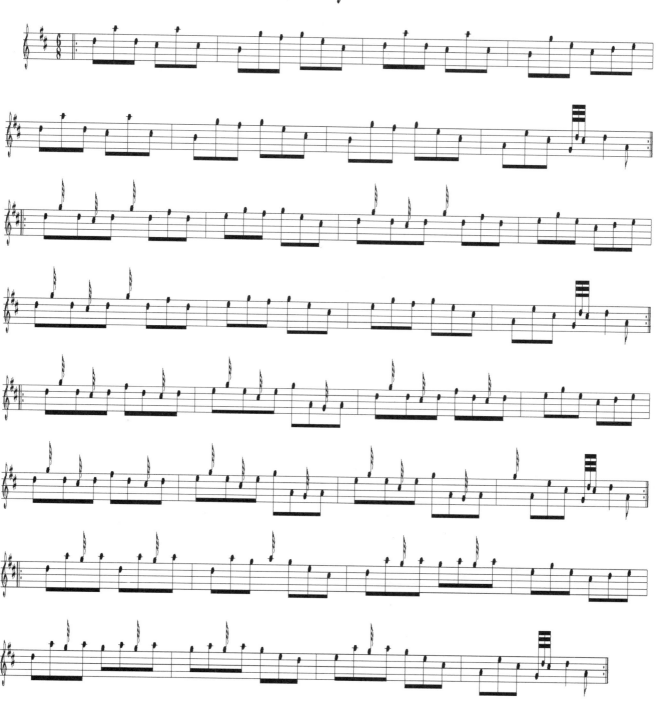

# The Custudian

14

# Da BOMSKWAD

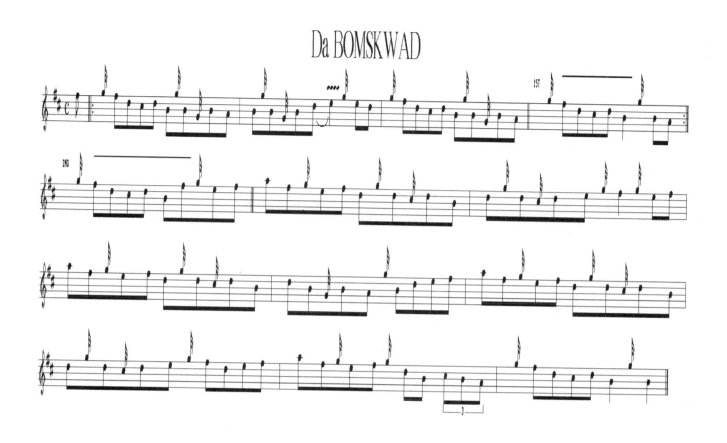

# Death Eats a Cracker

Death Eats a Cracker Parts 5/6

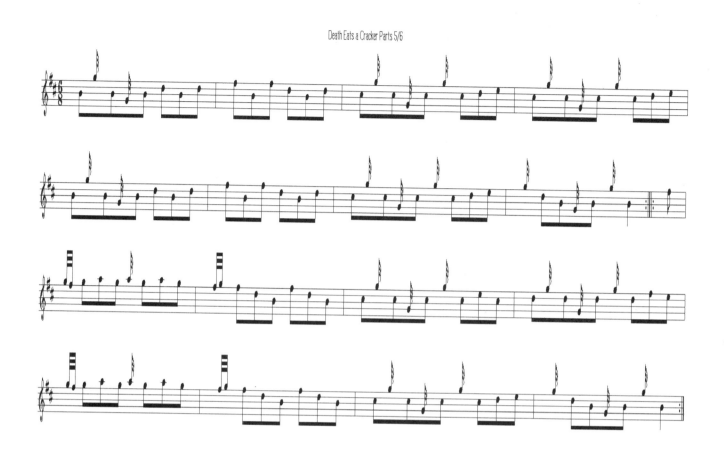

# Depression

# Driving Home

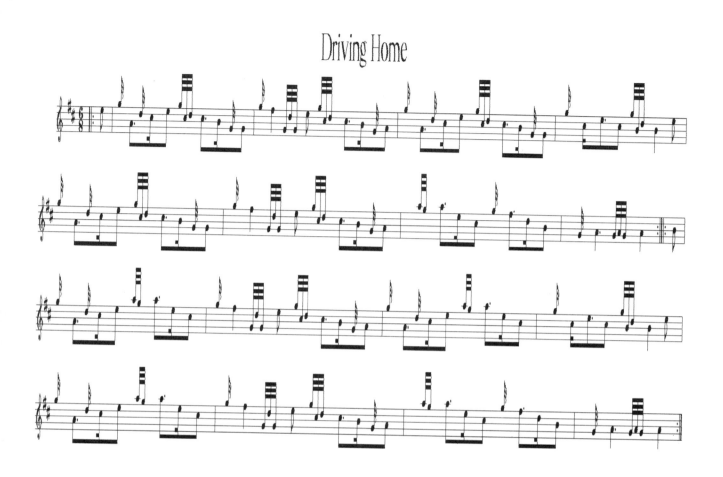

# Farewell the Long Chanter

# Going Out to Sea

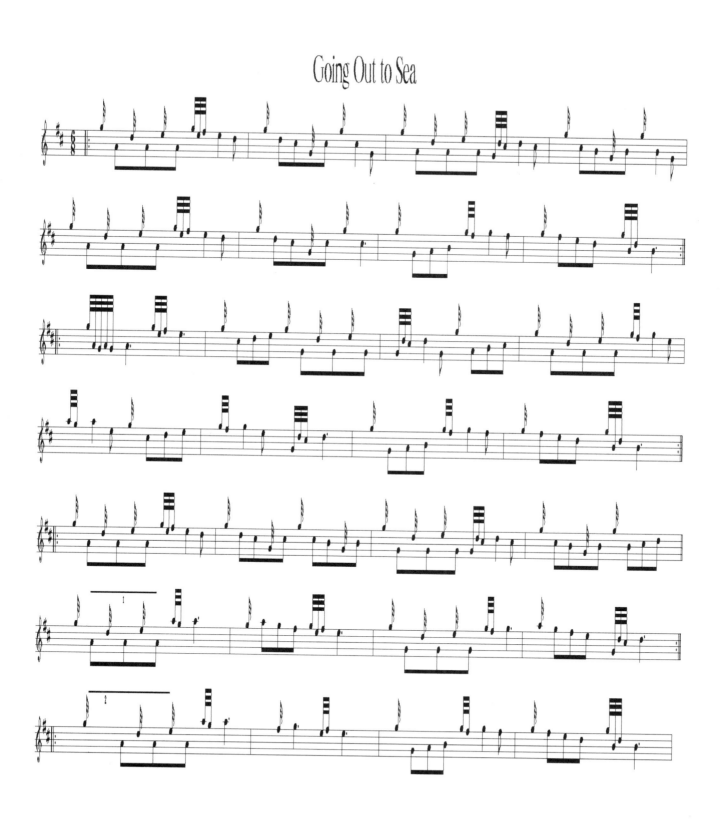

Going Out to Sea 4th Part

# Hampster Slayer

23

# The Hand That Rocks the Cradle

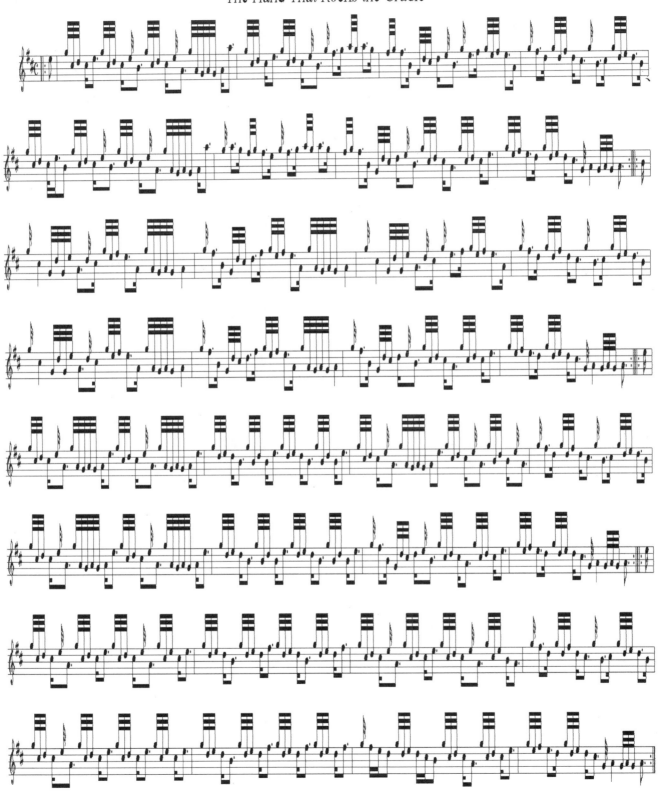

# Hands Across the Water

# Invercargill's Long Life

### 100 Years of Music

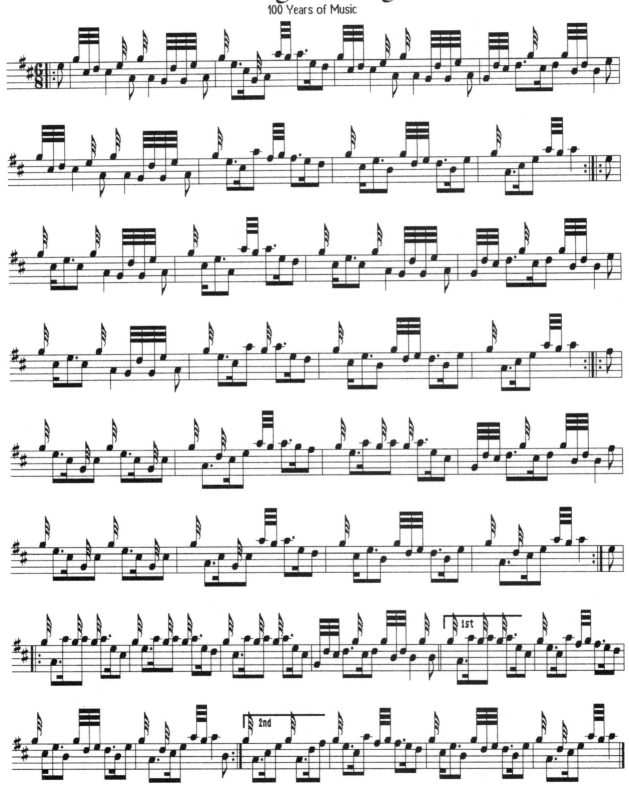

# Invercargill's Long Life

(Seconds)

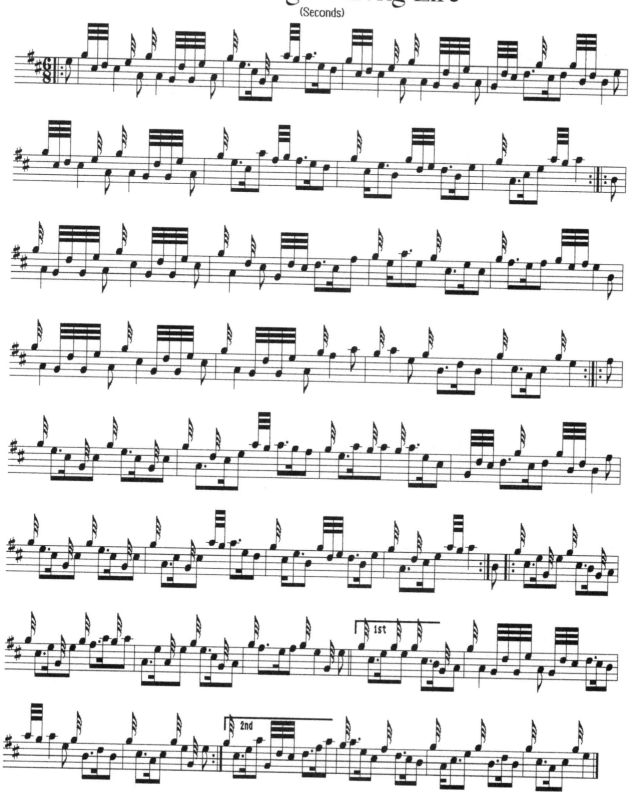

## Jimmy "Sticks" Moore

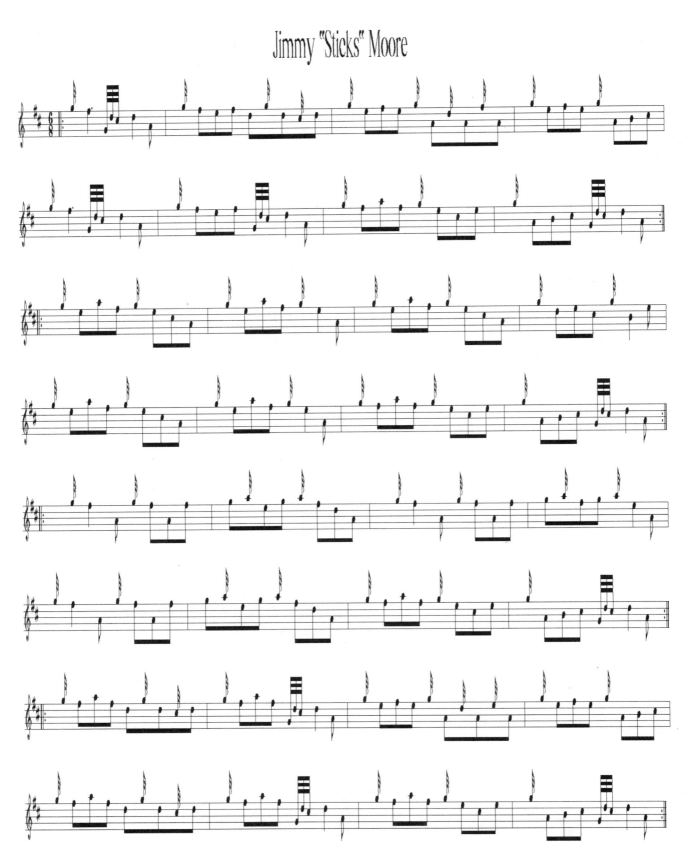

28

# Johnny B Drone

# Kill the Whistler

30

# Little Blue Bike

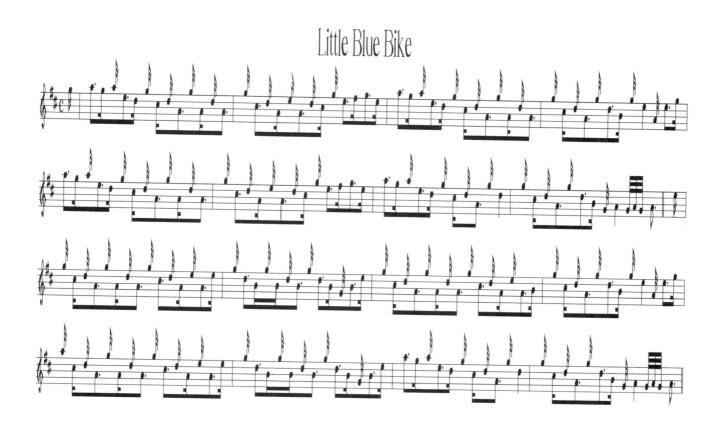

# The Locker Room

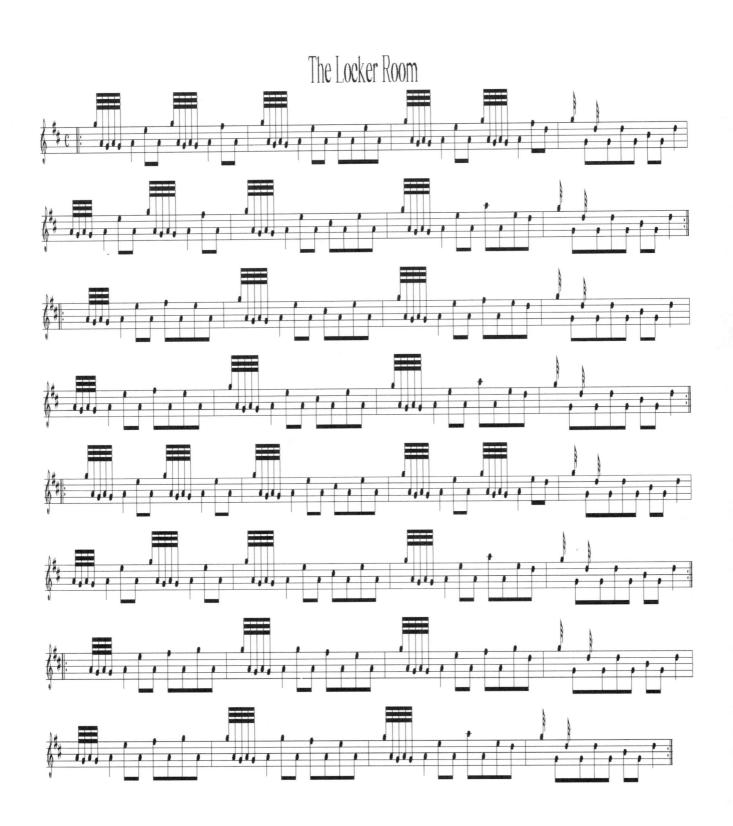

# Master's Last

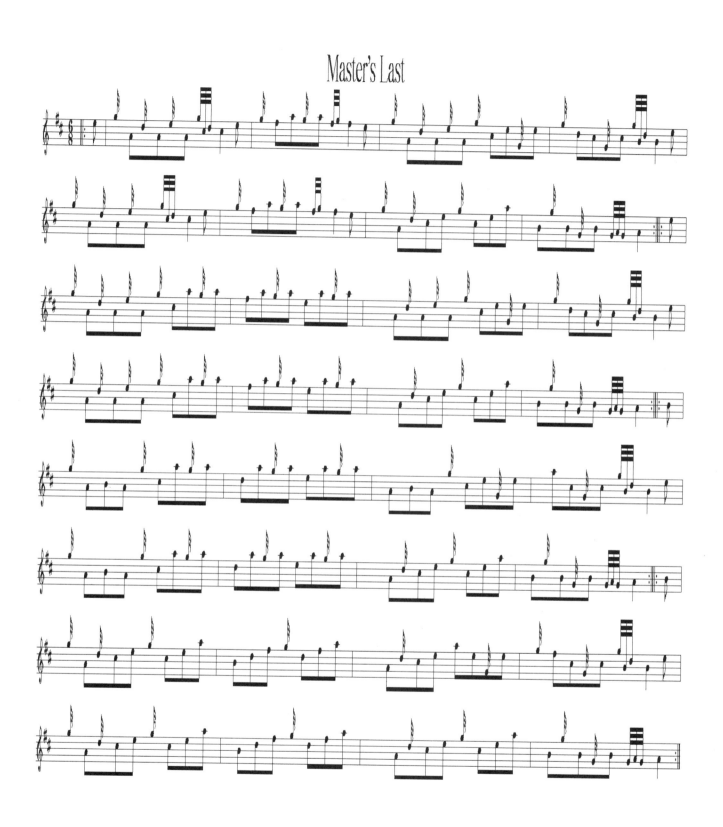

33

# The Mercury Slide

34

# Mike, It's Over...

# Offhand Reel

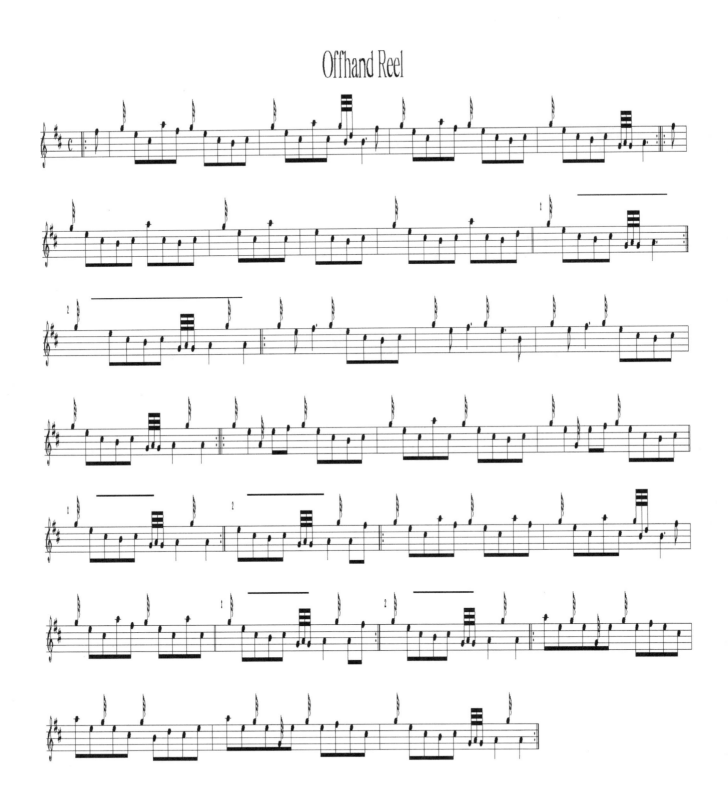

# Old Runners

# The Pipe Major's Complaint

38

The Pipe Major's Complaint Ending

# The Precipice

40

# The Precipice Seconds

# Pudgy Mary

42

# Rain on the Roof

# Remote Control

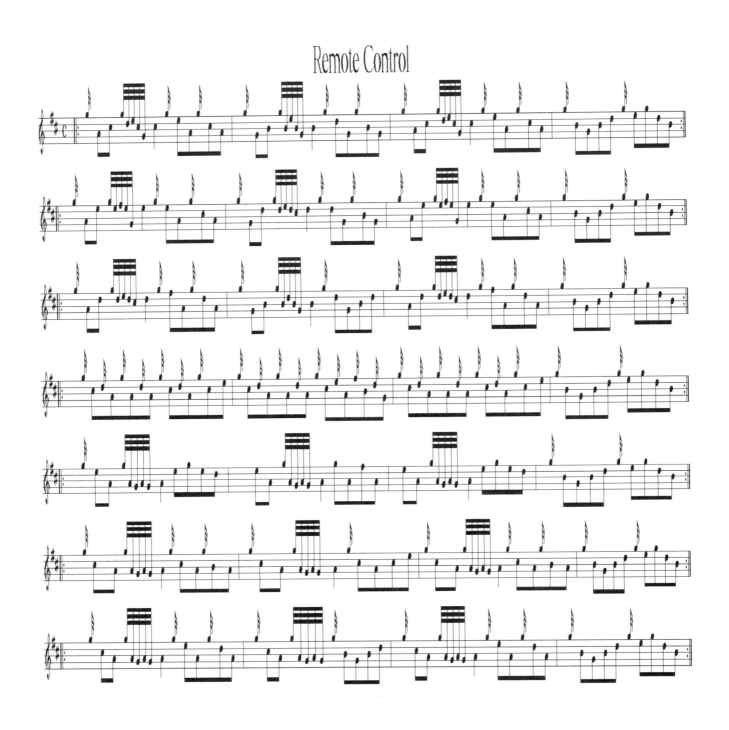

44

# The Resignation

# The Resignation Seconds

(For 3d and 4th Parts)

46

# Royal Red

# Season's End

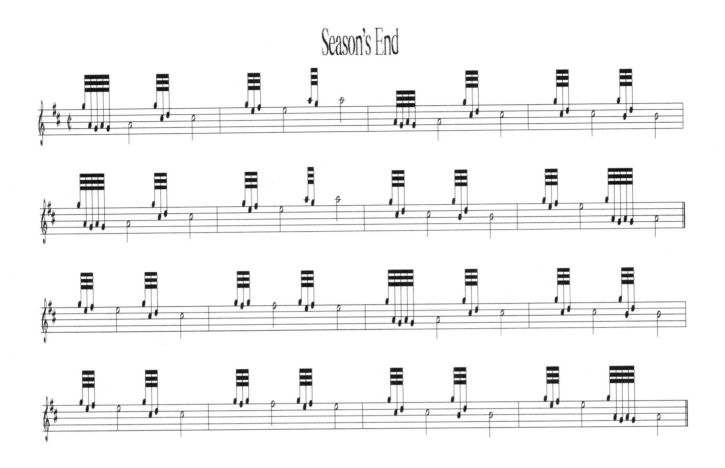

# Season's End Seconds

49

# Shetland Foxhunt

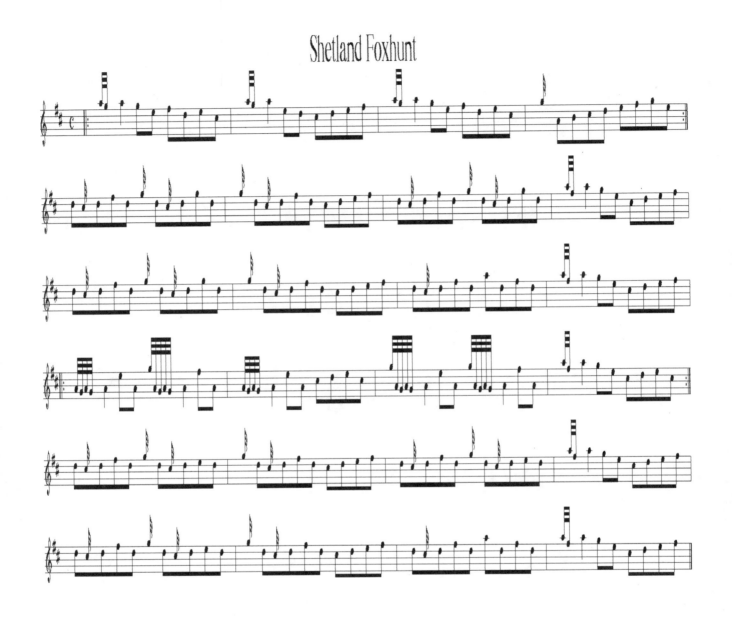

50

# Sodbusters

# The Tailor's Needle

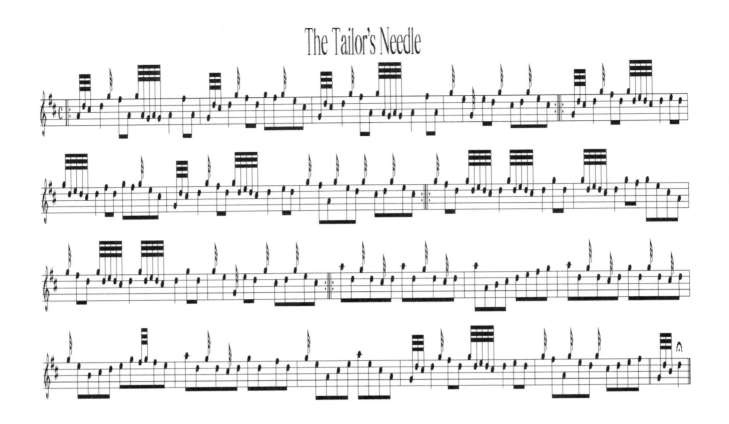

52

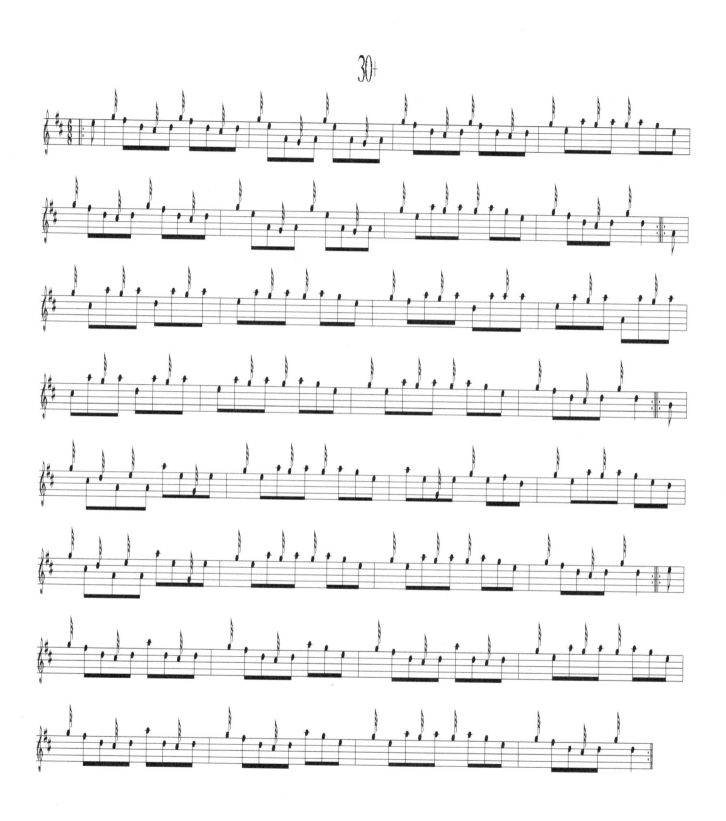

30+

53

# Tonka Bay

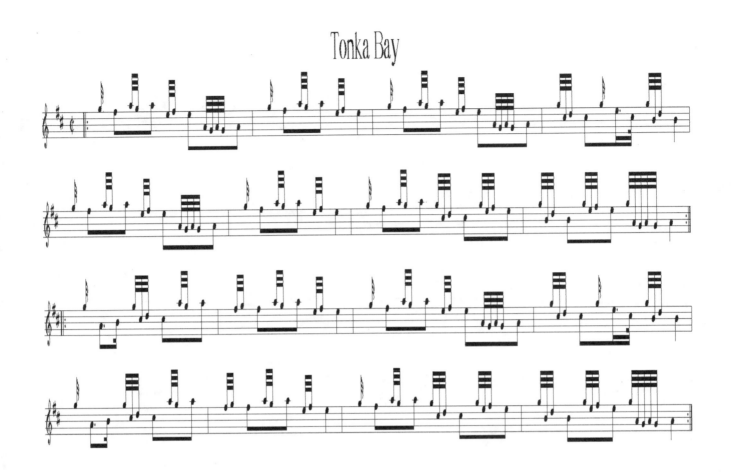

54

# The Top and Bottom Hand

# Twisted Finger

56

# Wilting in the Sun

57

# Wring My Mop

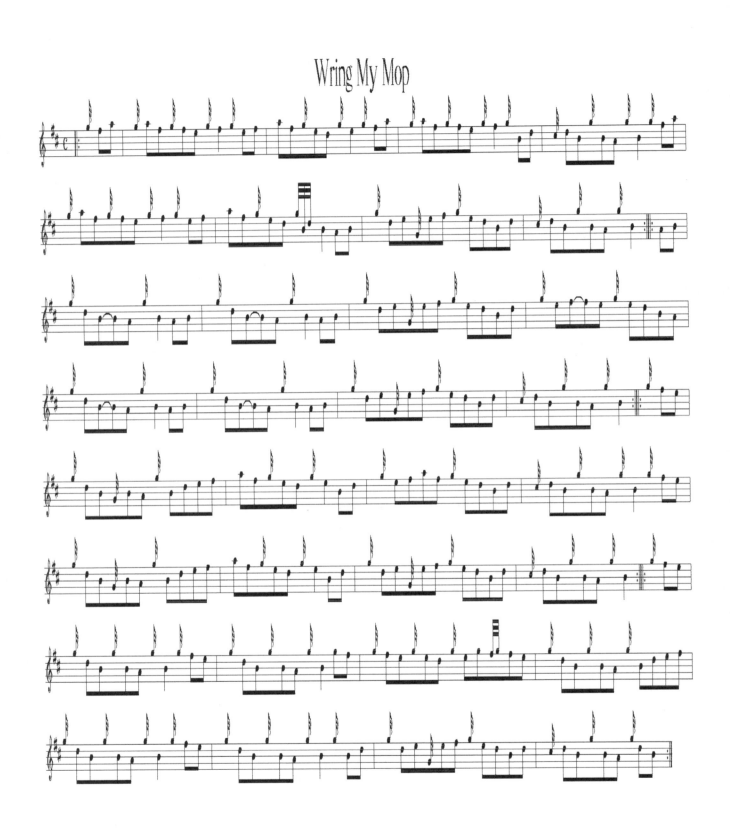

58

# Arrangements

# Cork Hill

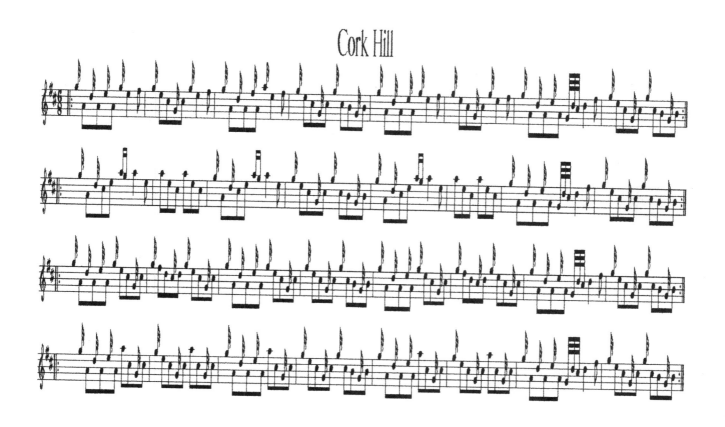

# The Foxhunter

# The Foxhunter

### (Seconds)

# Gilbert Clancy's Jig

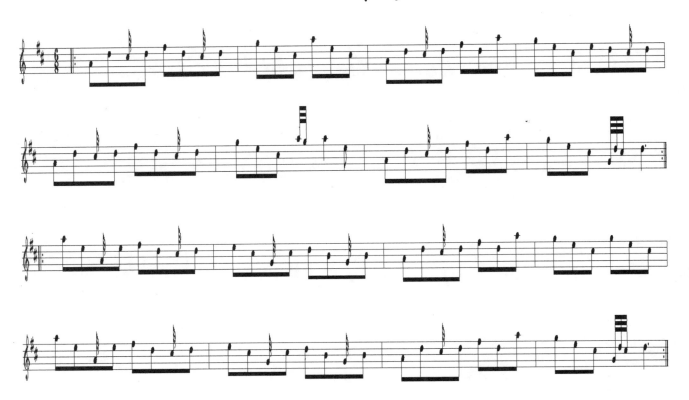

# The Hairy Marriers

(Birl City Reel)

# The Hairy Marriers 1st Harmony

(Birl City Reel)

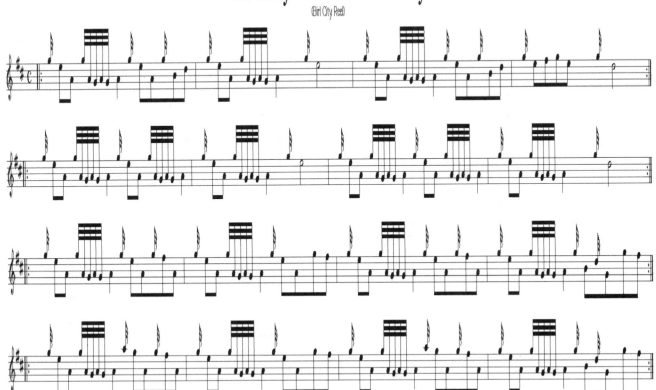

# The Hairy Marriers 2nd Harmony
(Birl City Reel)

# High Level

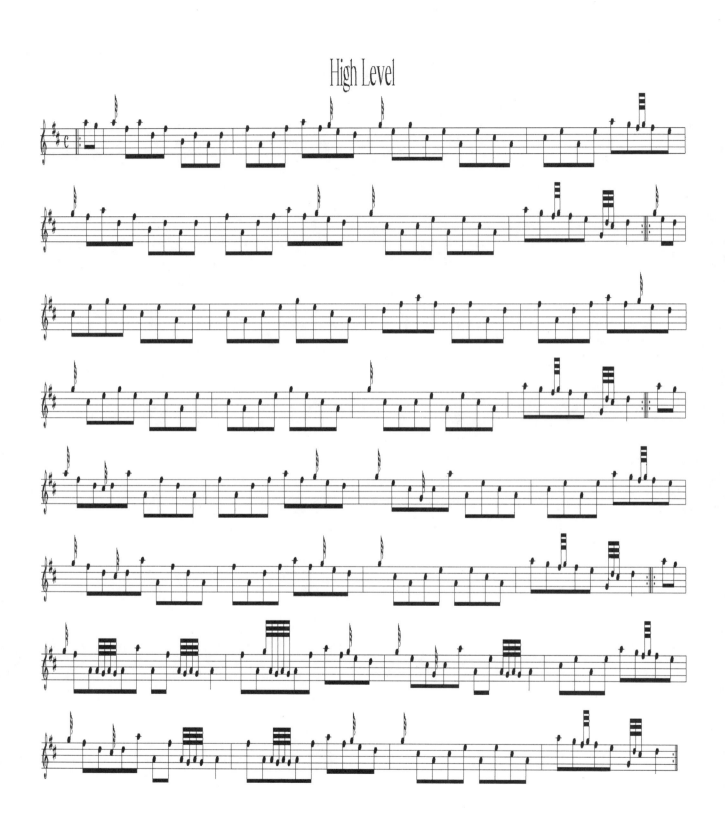

# Highland Laddie

# Highland Laddie

## (Seconds)

# Jock MacNichol's Fancy

# Scotland the Brave

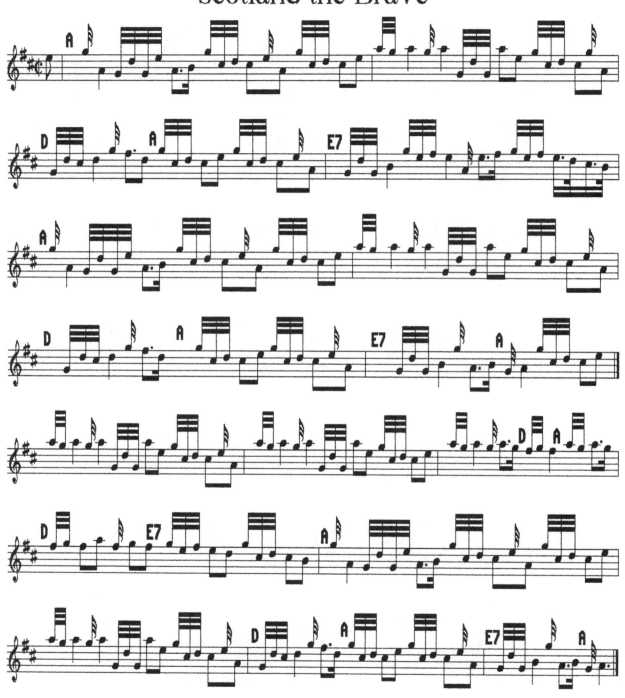

74

# Scotland the Brave

(Seconds)

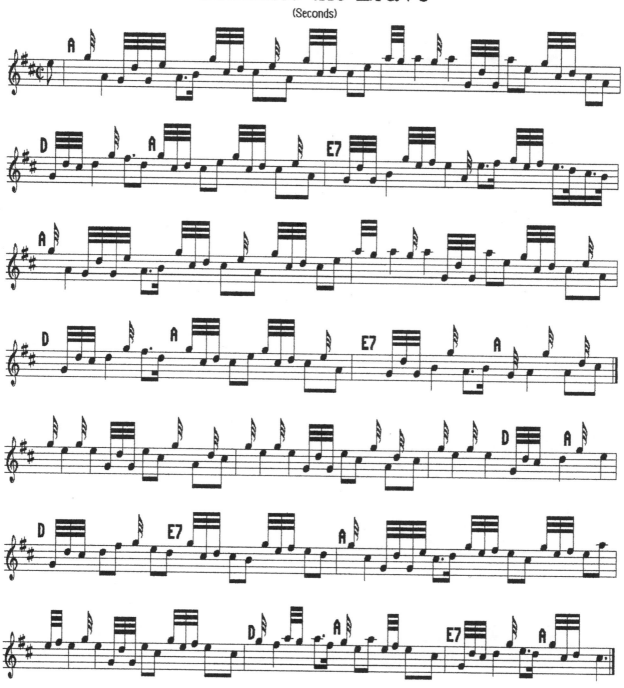

# Order Form

**Three Ways to Order:**

| **Mail** | **FAX** | **On-line** |
|---|---|---|
| The Shetland Piper | (612) 588-4372 | www.wavetech.net/~shetland |
| P.O. BOX 22663 | | |
| Robbinsdale, MN 55412-2663 | | |

**Books available from The Shetland Piper:**

The Pipe Major's Handbook, 2nd Edition   $19.95
The Zetland Tunebook, Volume 1   $14.95
The Lerwick Zetland Pipes Opperators Manual   $7.95

**Shipping**
$4.00 for the first book and $2.00 for each aditional book.

**Sales Tax**
Minnesota residents please add 6.5%.

**Payment**
☐Check
Credit Card:   ☐Visa   ☐MasterCard   ☐AMEX

Card Number_____ Exp Date_____
Name on Card_____

Name_____
Address_____
City_____ State_____ Zip_____
Phone_____ E-mail_____

Please see our website for more information.

# Order Form

## Three Ways to Order:

| Mail | FAX | On-line |
|------|-----|---------|
| The Shetland Piper | (612) 588-4372 | www.wavetech.net/~shetland |
| P.O. BOX 22663 | | |
| Robbinsdale, MN 55412-2663 | | |

## Books available from The Shetland Piper:

The Pipe Major's Handbook, 2nd Edition   $19.95
The Zetland Tunebook, Volume 1   $14.95
The Lerwick Zetland Pipes Opperators Manual   $7.95

## Shipping

$4.00 for the first book and $2.00 for each aditional book.

## Sales Tax

Minnesota residents please add 6.5%.

## Payment

☐Check
Credit Card:   ☐Visa   ☐MasterCard   ☐AMEX

Card Number_____ Exp Date_____
Name on Card_____

Name_____
Address_____
City_____State_____ Zip_____
Phone_____ E-mail_____

Please see our website for more information.